FIRE TRUCKS
IN ACTION

George Hall

Motorbooks International
Publishers & Wholesalers

In memory of Philadelphia Firefighter Vencent C. Acey,
Rescue 1 and Firefighter John J. Redmond, Ladder 11,
who died in action at Box 449, 28 January 1994.

First published in 1994 by Motorbooks International
Publishers & Wholesalers, PO Box 2, 729 Prospect Avenue,
Osceola, WI 54020 USA

Motorbooks International books are also available at discounts
in bulk quantity for industrial or sales-promotional use. For
details write to Special Sales Manager at the Publisher's address

Library of Congress Cataloging-in-Publication Data Available

ISBN 0-87938-927-3

On the front cover: Several brick industrial buildings going top-
to-bottom in a 5-11 fire on Orleans Street near the Chicago
River. Chicago substitutes the number eleven for the word
alarm; no one is quite sure why. It's probably a holdover from
the days of telegraphic communication among companies.
Tower Ladder 10 is an Emergency-One truck with a pre-
plumbed 1000gpm nozzle in the bucket. *Larry Shapiro photo*

On the frontispiece: The Chicago Fire Department's four squad
companies are the equivalent of heavy rescues in other cities.
They run in these small Snorkel trucks instead of traditional
rescue boxes. Other truckmen occasionally man the squad
buckets at large jobs to throw some more water while the
rescuemen are in the close-up firefight. *Larry Shapiro photo*

On the title page: San Francisco's Truck 15, a Spartan/LTI 100-
footer, is typical of the city's 18 tillered aerials. The SFFD runs
no other ladder types. Note Frisco's famous wooden hand
ladders, all custom-crafted in the city's shops.

On the back cover: Third alarm in Boston's Roxbury district. A
Boston third gets seven engines, five ladders, a rescue
company, the city's one tower ladder, and an assortment of
chiefs and special-call apparatus. The Special Unit, center, is
an Emergency-One lighting plant that rolls on all multiple-
alarm jobs.

Printed and bound in Hong Kong

Contents

Acknowledgments

Fire rigs are magnificent beasts, much beloved by the people who build and operate them. A lot of folks helped us gather photos and information for this book— far too many to mention by name. As the saying goes, you know who you are. Thanks to all for the generous help.

We tried for a mix of real-life action shots as well as the pretty but static poses— the noble fire engine out standing in its field. But the working shots are tough; things just never seem to happen when the photographer is in town. It's always the same line: "Geez, you shoulda been here last week, the joint was jumpin'." Although the fire buffs hate it, the fact is that fire incidents are down, way down, everywhere in America. It's good news for the citizenry, but a drag for fire fans. Lots of factors are at work: better building codes, more sprinklers and alarm systems, greater conscious-ness of prevention, fewer people smoking. Smoking in bed used to be good for several jobs a night in the big cities. Still, we caught good "workers" in Chicago, New York, San Francisco, Phoenix, and New England, among other places. We'll keep chasing the box for future books.

As always there are a few people who deserve special mention for going above and beyond in an effort to help us out. Heartfelt thanks to Bob Milnes in Miami, Byron Rhodes in Orlando, Chief Bob Oden in Phoenix, Commissioners Leo Stapleton and Marty "The Coach" Pierce in Boston, Jack Calderone at *Fire Apparatus Journal*, Evert Wilson in Las Vegas, Chief Don Hein-buch in Baltimore, plus Creed Ray and the boys on Munjoy Hill in Portland, Maine. And we shouldn't forget Galen Thomaier at the "Last Resort Fire Department" in Seat-tle, one of the most amazing private apparatus collections anywhere. This outfit deserves a book all its own.

Your author took most but not all of the pictures. Some of the best fire photographers in the business are represented, including Tom Wanstall, John Cetrino, Mike Delaney at the Providence *Journal*, Joel Woods, and Larry Shapiro. Their shots are credited separately. I couldn't have made it come together without them.

George Hall
Tiburon, California
April 1994

A Brief History

Modern fire engines and trucks are complex battlewagons, ready to swing into all-out action with zero notice. These amazing rigs have undergone an evolution process three centuries long, the first hand-operated pump wagons having made their appearance in the late 1600s. Although several waves of industrialization and technology have washed over fire apparatus development in those three centuries, the basic principles haven't changed much: 1) mobilize rapidly from a position of complete preparedness; 2) search the building and remove potential victims; 3) open up the building to vent heat and gases; and 4) put water on the flames. The order depends on the situation.

People discovered a long time ago, way back before recorded history began, that plain old water did a good job of dousing fire. It is still the foremost firefighting tool,

although it is sometimes mixed with various wetting, foaming, or sticking agents to increase effectiveness with particular types of fire. We probably remember the so-called "fire triad" from high school science classes. Fire needs three elements to survive and prevail: fuel, oxygen, and heat or combustion. Water efficiently attacks two legs of the triad, by separating oxygen from the fuel and by lowering temperatures. Given enough water, a fire of any size can be doused.

The earliest fire "engines" were nothing but troughs on wheels, with rows of leather buckets to convey the water to the seat of the fire. The next development was the

Classic San Francisco red on a perfectly restored 1938 Fageol pumper, now privately owned by Richard Stacks. Fageols were built in Oakland, California, in the 1930s.

wheeled hand pump, whose levers or "brakes" were manned by eager volunteers while other firefighters got water onto the flames via fabric hose. By the mid-nineteenth century urban volunteer companies manned hand pumpers that had room for forty stalwarts on four sets of brakes, and the rigs could throw a stream into a window several stories high. But hand pumps soon exhausted even the fittest crews, and huge pools of manpower were required to keep the hose streams flowing.

But this was the Age of Steam, and locomotive manufacturers soon branched out into the business of building steam fire engines that could be pulled by horses. In this day and age we forget what a tremendously powerful energy source steam can be; in the late 1800s train engines were pulling mile-long freight columns at 90 miles per hour, and the largest fire pumpers were moving water at volumes and pressures greater than many modern diesel rigs can manage. The six-ton monsters built by Amoskeag and Silsby could pump 1400 gallons per minute at 100 psi pressures for as long as water and coal supplies held out. For the first time in human history man had at hand a technology for putting truly serious amounts of water onto a structure fire.

The steam-powered fire engines had another revolutionary effect. No longer was there a reliance on platoons of volunteers to drag the rig through the streets and man the pump handles. The steam pumper could fight fire all day and night with a crew of two: a driver and a fireman to stoke the boiler. As the steam apparatus became the norm in American cities, so did the paid professional fire department. Most big US cities switched from volunteer to paid departments in the years immediately after the Civil War.

Steam rigs were typically pulled by three large horses conditioned to function fearlessly at fire scenes. The rigs were so heavy that their hoses, nozzles, tools and coal were carried in a second wagon. The firemen occasionally rode the hose wagon to the fire, but in most departments they were expected to run behind the apparatus to the job! In fact, the first small steamers were hand-pulled, horses being enormously expensive to maintain.

Response times for horse-drawn companies were astonishingly quick, even by present-day standards. In an 1875 demonstration for visiting royalty, a Brooklyn engine turned out to the bell, hitched up the horses, rode three blocks to a mock "job," led to a hydrant, and pumped a good hose stream in just under three minutes. The horses were hitched to the rigs with quick-fastening harnesses that dropped from the ceiling, and the engine's fireman kept hot water in the boiler 24 hours a day via quick-disconnect copper connections to the station's heating plant. The fireman would light off the kerosene-soaked kindling before going out the door, and he could be seen stoking the steam plant from

Engine 1 from Avon, Massachusetts, a classic New York-style Mack, supplies big-time water to a tower ladder at a warehouse fire in the southern suburbs of Boston. *John Cetrino photo*

the back step as the engine careened to the job at 20 miles per hour. Fire steamers had water-in-tube boilers that could build usable steam pressure in only a few minutes.

Other horse-drawn wagons, called "trucks" or "hook-and-ladders," accompanied the engines to the fire and set to work handling rescues and venting. This division of firefighting labor, first worked out in colonial Philadelphia, is the norm in all parts of the world today. A word about correct nomenclature: a "fire engine" is the rig that pumps the water, and a "fire truck" is the larger vehicle that carries ladders, rescue tools, and other heavy gear. Most engines run with one small ladder for emergencies, but most trucks have no mechanism for putting water on a fire other than hand extinguishers or pump cans. Engines are also called "pumpers" or, in countries once connected with England, "motors." Some departments refer to their trucks as "ladders." No rhyme or reason here: in Boston, Minneapolis and Honolulu they're "ladders"; in Chicago, Dallas and San Francisco they're "trucks." The word "apparatus" can refer to any firefighting vehicle from rescue squad to fireboat. In England they like the word "appliance."

Trucks also took on sophistication and capability along with the steam pumpers. In the late 19th century many cities ran aerial ladder trucks with wooden "sticks" that could be raised by huge springs or by cranks and worms. Of course a selection of hand ladders, some as long as 65 feet, was also available on the typical hook-and-ladder. Companion rigs, known as water towers, could also be special-called to big blazes. With a steam engine leading to the tower, its high-volume nozzle could be raised hydraulically as high as 75 feet above the street and a powerful 900 gallon-per-minute stream could be directed with great precision into a particular window. Photos of New York's dreadful Triangle Shirtwaist fire in 1911 show two American LaFrance towers blasting powerful master streams into the remains of the tenth-floor sweatshop. They were clearly knocking the hell out of the fire, but too late to save the 112 immigrant seamstresses who jumped to their deaths. Cities like San Francisco were so attached to their towers that they towed them with modern Ahrens-Fox gasoline trucks and put them to work well into the 1950s. There is a restored beauty in Frisco's fire museum, built by a local tower and nozzle manufacturer called Gorter. Some of the first self-propelled fire rigs were existing pumpers and ladders attached to steam or gas tractors.

Apparatus designed around gasoline engines became common in the years right before World War I. The fire lads, ever the traditionalists, hated to give up their beloved horses, but it was obvious to all that the time had come. Gas rigs could handle the hills, they could speed over great distances, they could lug far more weight. And operating costs plummeted;

horseflesh was expensive to maintain. The beasts had to be fed and cared for constantly, even though the companies seldom got more than a few calls a day. For some reason the years 1922–23 were the last for the horses in several dozen American fire departments, from San Francisco to New York. Phildadelphia hung on determinedly but irrationally until 1929.

It is interesting that the engines and trucks of today do almost the same jobs as their horsedrawn counterparts of a century ago. The big differences aren't found in the realms of gallons-per-minute or ladder heights, but rather in the areas of speed, reliability, and firefighter safety. They are also equipped to do a whole lot more than throw a stream on a fire or a ladder to the roof. Most American fire departments also run as first responders on medical emergencies, backing up city ambulance crews, and today's typical rig carries a selection of first-aid gear. Toxic cleanup is another big concern in the '90s, and firefighting companies are expected to take on these unpleasant messes along with dedicated hazardous-materials ("haz-mat") compa-

nies. And it's the fire department that is called to help out with heavy rescues, extrications at auto accidents, industrial mishaps, cave-ins, mass-transit wrecks, people stuck in elevators, water disasters—you name it. In the mid-'90s it has reached the point in most American cities where fewer than a third of total "runs" are fire calls.

That alarm is more likely a heart attack, a car wreck, a water leak. People call on their firefighters to help them in every conceivable situation, and the firefighters go willingly.

But the eye of the needle in all departments is preparedness. The people have to be trained for any eventuality, and the rigs have to be properly equipped to respond and set to work with absolutely no notice. It's not enough to throw the gear into the truck; it has to be stowed in its proper place, and it has to be ready for action with no arguments. That means power saws oiled and gassed, batteries charged, booster tanks filled, hose lengths folded and coiled with precision. Everything has to work perfectly every time; anything less is unthinkable.

Chapter 1

Engines

Firefighters everywhere engage in friendly banter about engine work versus truck work. It's usually the truckmen who have the honor of making the "saves," or rescues from within the burning building. They also ladder the windows to provide multiple exit paths. Once they've searched, they're up to the roof to open doorway-sized holes so that the heat, smoke and gases in the building can rise and escape. It's classic firefighting work, requiring courage and physical stamina in equal abundance.

The engine guys, of course, pooh-pooh these arguments. As far as they're concerned, firefighting is concentrated at the tip of the sword. In New York they call it the "nob." It's the nozzle at the end of a high-pressure hose line.

If you're not on the nob, facing down the Red Devil at arm's length, then you're missing all the fun. The typical engineman will climb over his mother to take the line and put "the wet stuff on the red stuff." As the Red Baron said about flying fighters in the Great War, "All else, lads, is rubbish."

Modern American fire engines are much alike everywhere in the country. Most are powered by diesel engines that put about 350 horsepower to the wheels. This same powerplant drives the internal pump, and the typical rig throws anywhere from 1250 to 2000 gallons per minute through one or several hose leads. The engine's main job is pumping water, but many departments task engine crews with medical first-aid duties as well. It's increasingly more common for urban engines to carry basic life support (BLS) medical gear, including resus-

One of south Chicago's many E-One engines is left pumping at a South Side church fire.
Larry Shapiro photo

citation bottles and electronic defibrillators for serious cardiac problems. Some cities even run extended-cab engines that have room in the back for enclosed patient treatment and transport.

Engine manning (or person-ing, since most US departments now hire women firefighters) varies widely, from a solo driver to the New York City high figure of an officer plus five firefighters. For years the ideal figure was five—a driver who would stay with the rig at the job to run the pump, and two two-man teams who could advance separate lines on the fire. Most cities these days run their pumpers with

The Phoenix FD's Engine 9 arrives first-due at a high-rise job north of downtown. The rig is an Emergency-One 1500gpm pumper with air conditioning—a must in a desert city where temperatures are routinely above 100 degrees.

crews of three or four.

The typical US engine, regardless of manufacturer, is referred to as a "triple combination." In the horse-drawn days, the steamer ran with a second wagon carrying hose and tools. When the first gasoline engines combined these functions onto one chassis, they were called "double combinations." An engine becomes a "triple" with the addition of an internal water tank for ultra-rapid fire attacks without a hydrant hook-up. The typical booster tank holds 500 gallons, although some engines carry as much as 1000 gallons—three tons of dead weight.

In rare and drastic cases an engine crew will elect to hit a big inside fire directly from the booster supply, relying on the engine's driver to hook them up to good hydrant pressure before the tank runs dry. With a 300gpm lead the 500-gallon tank will last less than two minutes, so the chauffeur/pump operator has to know his stuff. Says Boston engine driver John Cetrino, "You never, never want to let that tank run dry at a job. The best thing that can happen is embarrassment and maybe engine damage; the diesel will shriek when there's suddenly nothing to pump. Everybody will hear it, and they'll be ribbing your ass for weeks. The worst thing that can happen is a dead engine crew, if they're caught inside and woops, no water." Commonly the booster tank is used for small rubbish fires and fuel wash-downs. Many rigs have a separate rubber hose reel for use

Miami's Hose 2, a 1250gpm Young, sports
unusual compressed-air bus doors on either side
of the crew compartment.

only with the tank.

There are quad combinations and quint combinations as well; we'll take a look at these interesting rigs later in the book. Quads are part-engine and part truck. They carry an array of ground ladders as well as pump, hose, and tank. The quint, popular with many smaller departments, adds a powered aerial ladder or water tower to the mix.

The fire engine is only as good as its water supply. Most cities have extensive underground water systems exclusively for firefighting use. Above-ground hydrants, often color-coded to show different pressure levels, are found on almost every corner, so the engine will never have to drop more than a few hundred feet of line to get water onto the fire. Most engines keep a short hydrant jumper pre-connected to the main intake valve, which is usually on the rig's nose. Attack lines of different diameters are likewise pre-connected and "flaked" or folded in the rear hose bed, where they can be yanked out and put to work in seconds. A good pump operator can roll the rig up to a hydrant, hook up the jumper, move to the controls at the midship control panel, manipulate the gates, and supply water to the attack lines in one minute. That's if the hydrant is con-

Port Everglades, the container and petroleum terminal north of Ft. Lauderdale, runs a trio of awesome Mack foam tankers nicknamed "Puff," "Snuff" (shown), and "Enough."

The author's home town of Tiburon ("Great White Shark" in Spanish) is just over the Golden Gate bridge from San Francisco. Its small paid department relies on a matched pair of Pierce Dash engines, one a 1986 and the other a 1989. Both are 1250gpm models with 500-gallon booster tanks. Each is manned by a crew of two, with volunteers taking up the slack at working fires. The Wisconsin manufacturer was unheard-of on the West Coast a decade ago, but aggressive marketing and a superb product line have combined to place several hundred rigs in service west of the Rockies.

Matchless over-the-road truck manufacturer Kenworth is based in Seattle, and they have delved into the world of fire apparatus from time to time. These conventional-snout pumpers were built for the Seattle Fire Department in the early '70s, and a few are still in front-line service. This handsome number runs at "Twenty-Sixes." Don't ask why, but everyone in the SFD pluralizes all stations in normal conversations: "I work at Sevens; he's switching to the truck at Thirteens," etc. Fire departments are full of this kind of arcane weirdness.

veniently located. Often it's not; half the time it's across the street, for instance.

Engines can also draw, or "draft," water from lakes or bays through a hard-suction tube that can be lowered from a dock or pier. This is an excellent alternative in the event of failing water pressure in a city hydrant system, and most engine companies go to the shore and drill with the hard-suction line from time to time. In the 1989 San Francisco earthquake the hydrant mains in the Marina district were wrecked by the earth movement, and several big structure fires had to be fought with water

Springfield, Oregon, across Interstate 5 from Eugene, is the only department with orange rigs now that Baltimore is switching back to red. This great-looking new Pierce quint sports a 75 foot SQURT ladder tower with a permanently mounted 1000gpm motorized Akron nozzle. The town deals with a considerable fire hazard from the many lumber mills and yards nearby.

drawn from the bayfront a half mile away. The city's fireboat was the primary pumping source, the sea water being moved through an above-ground portable hydrant system designed for this exact emergency.

San Francisco suffered a similar failure of its firefighting mains in the far larger 1906 earthquake, and most of the city was lost to fire. Today the SFFD can also make use of underground cisterns in fifty locations around the city, each holding as much as a million gallons. An engine crew

Around back at the job pictured on the back cover. Engine 28 is setting up to supply water to the Tower Unit. The BFD is big on ladder work, with a forest of aerial sticks and hand ladders going up at almost every good job.

needs only to drop their hard line through a specially marked manhole, and they'll be assured of water for hours of firefighting.

The typical fire engine carries hose lengths ranging from the small-diameter rubber reel, used for nuisance fires, to heavy hand lines of 3in diameter. The normal attack line is a 1 1/2in or 1 3/4in lead; a single firefighter can easily handle the nob on the end of these smaller lines, although his arm and shoulder muscles will be crying the blues after about 15 minutes. Different departments swear by various nozzle designs. New York's enginemen tend to like old-style brass tips that put a narrow, precise stream into the heart of the fire. Other departments use high-dispersion fog nozzles that provide wider coverage and greater heat protection for the men on the nob. But everyone agrees on the importance of moving in on the fire, finding its seat, and knocking the hell out of it before it expands to hopeless proportions.

Most pumpers also pack a high-volume nozzle, often called a monitor or deck gun, that can throw out more than 1000gpm from a position atop the rig. Many engines used to have two. Deck guns are often

Now this is what a fire engine is supposed to look like! Unique Seagrave snout from the '50s can be seen echoed in the newest V-8 Ram pickup trucks from Dodge. The grand old Centre Hanover, Massachusetts, Engine 14 is now in the loving hands of a private collector, and restoration is ongoing.

The new Emergency-One pumper out of Bridgewater, Massachusetts, is supplying water to Easton's ancient Pirsch snub-nose aerial for ladder pipe operations at a general alarm in Taunton. You have to love Bridgewater's motto on all their apparatus: "We Protect And Conquer."

mounted on a steel plate and held down by wing nuts so they can be lifted off the engine and set up in the street for master-stream operations. Switching to deck guns usually signals an abandonment of the inside firefight in favor of a safer outside attack, known in firefighting as the old "surround and drown" technique.

A notable exception: Boston's recently retired Captain Elliott "Deck Gun" Miller was infamous for putting Blue Hill Avenue Engine 52's gun to work on everything from dumpster fires on up, and for refusing to call in additional help regardless of the fire's volume! (Fire Alarm: "Engine 52, whaddya got there?" Deck Gun Miller:

Chicago's Engine 91, an E-One, pumps merrily
away under sub-zero conditions at a third alarm
on Devon Avenue. *Larry Shapiro photo*

New York loves its Mack pumpers, although it flirts from time to time with American LaFrance and other marques. Many neighboring cities, like Yonkers immediately north of the Bronx, purchase gear with the same specs as the FDNY. Piggy-backed orders save money for everyone. *Tom Wanstall photo*

"This is 52, we got a three-story frame vacant, fire on all floors, deck gun in operation." The engine's pump can be heard screaming at max rpm in the background. Fire Alarm: "Geez, you want we should strike the box?" Deck Gun: "Nah, 52 can handle.")

Several American cities have experimented over the years with "super-pumpers" that move huge amounts of water from high-volume water systems or from waterfront drafts. The FDNY used to operate a gigantic pump on a Mack semi-truck chassis; its Howitzer-sized gun, carried on a companion rig, could literally put a water stream through a brick wall, and a fleet of hose tenders laid its special 5in lines from the fire to the water source. New

San Francisco's Engine 36 runs all-out at a fifth alarm, putting 900gpm through the deck gun and another 600 gallons into a collection of hand lines.

York still fields several so-called "satellite" engines with smaller versions of the old Super Pumper water cannon.

Engines also carry assorted clean-up and rescue gear for forcible entry, protection from water damage, and overhauling operations after the fire is out. A small extension ladder, good for perhaps 18 feet, is available but rarely used. And self-contained breathing apparatus, one tank for each firefighter, can be spotted on every

Two depressed mill towns near Boston, Lowell and Lawrence, have staggered under tremendous fire loads in recent years. Lowell's small paid department (eight engines and four ladder trucks) handled more than 200 working fires in 1993. *John Cetrino photo*

modern fire engine. The typical bottle provides about 30 minutes of air under normal working conditions. It's hard to believe that as recently as thirty years ago firefighters thought nothing of entering desperate inside firefights without any sort of breathing protection. Now all enlightened departments insist on masks for everyone in prac-

tically any smoke or hazardous-materials environment. Some of the old-timers still show disdain for the breathing gear, considering mask use somehow unmanly. Chiefs and company officers have to watch the tough nuts to ensure 100 percent compliance.

The typical engineman will climb over his mother to take the line and put "the wet stuff on the red stuff." As the Red Baron said about flying fighters in the Great War, "All else, lads, is rubbish."

Above
Open-cab Crown pumpers were the norm in southern California cities until only recently. This flat-nose with 1250gpm pump still serves the town of Covina, some 20 miles east of Los Angeles. *Joel Woods photo*

Right
No hurry today, boys; plenty of fire for everybody. San Francisco's Engine 29, an American LaFrance known as "Big Line 29," sets up for "surround and drown" operations with 3in lines and the deck gun.

Above

The engine driver runs the pump at the job, controlling rates and pressures through a variety of hose leads. He is responsible for rapid hook-up to a hydrant or other source and continuous supply at correct pressures to the hose crew inside the fire building.

Left

Emergency-One builds several lines of engines and tenders with conventional hoods, like this good-looking rescue pumper based on a Freightliner chassis. Some feature all-wheel drive. This 1993 model with 1250gpm pump works for the volunteer department in Solomans, MD. *Joel Woods photo*

San Francisco's Blackburn portable hydrant system, named after designer-inventor (and former SFFD division chief) Frank Blackburn, can move large volumes of water more than a mile in the event of earthquake damage to underground mains. The system performed brilliantly in the 1989 Loma Prieta earthquake, when fires in the Marina district raged unchecked because of shattered water systems. The Blackburn system with its 5in hose was used to shuttle water from the fireboat *Phoenix* anchored in the yacht harbor a half mile from the biggest of the fires. A trio of old hose tenders have been revamped to carry the SFFD's Blackburn hydrant system and several miles of 5in hose. Each tender also carries a high-volume (1200gpm) non-portable deck gun.

Chapter 2

Trucks

Engine companies can handle many smaller fires on their own. The truck companies join the fight when a real three-dimensional inside firefight develops. Truckmen don't worry much about water. They have other responsibilities, for which they're specially trained and equipped. They search the fire building for victims and for fire extension; they throw ladders to let firefighters in and residents out; they vent the structure by opening the roof and breaking out windows; and they evacuate neighboring exposure buildings if the fire appears to be spreading. Truck crews also handle large-volume water streams from the outside when the firefight takes a turn toward the hopeless.

Truck work is extremely physical, with lots of climbing, heavy lifting, and grueling searches under appalling heat and smoke conditions. As an unwritten rule most paid departments put their taller and huskier people on the ladders. The classic fire rescue—the unconscious victim being carried gingerly down the ladder through smoke and spray—is likely to be the work of a truckman.

Ladder truck crews can range from a solo driver to a high of seven firefighters on some New York trucks. Another FDNY refinement is the assignment of a specific job and position to each truckman. The chauffeur stays with the rig and operates the ladder or tower from the street. The officer initiates the inside search, accompanied by a two-man irons team carrying

Pierce 105 foot aerial gets a workout at a factory job in Skokie, a Chicago suburb to the north. The heavy-stream appliance permanently installed on the ladder can be remote-controlled by the operator on the turntable. *Larry Shapiro photo*

crowbar, Halligan and other forcible-entry tools. If the truck company has been assigned one or more new guys, or "probies," they'll be on the irons team so the company officer can keep them under his wing. More experienced firefighters will take the other slots: the roof man heads straight up the aerial to supervise venting from above, and the outside vent man works as a free agent on the interior stairwells or the fire escapes. Your writer refers to "men" since although the FDNY does have female firefighters, it tends to put them to work on engines rather than ladder trucks. New York also believes in lots and lots of portable radios—more so than any other department by far. In a typical truck company the officer, driver, roof man and vent man will each be on the air providing good intelligence for the chiefs leading the firefight. Good radio discipline is essential when there are so many units on a single channel. As they summarize in the FDNY: no speechmakers, no screamers.

Other departments are less strict with regard to truckwork assignments. Boston is famous for sophisticated ground ladder work, and it likes to field lots of truck companies—25 at last count. San Francisco's similar-sized department (1,500 people in round figures) runs 18 trucks by compari-

Nighttime second alarm, or 2-11, on Chicago's north side. Tower Ladder 23, foreground, is in rescue mode while companion Tower Ladder 39 sets up in the background for master-stream operations. *Larry Shapiro photo*

The classic fire rescue— the unconscious victim being carried gingerly down the ladder through smoke and spray—is likely to be the work of a truckman.

son. Boston truckmen go to work at the direction of their chiefs and their company officer, instead of moving off to a predetermined position. The driver of the truck, as in most departments, stays at the turntable to operate the stick.

And it's the truck crews everywhere that get stuck with one of the most unpleasant aspects of the job—overhauling. This is the careful check, after the fire is supposedly out, for hidden extension. Overhauling

Phoenix operates these enormous Spartan/LTI tillered aerials with 90 foot sticks and roll-up doors all around.

Right
Seattle's Truck 4 is another wonderful Kenworth conventional custom-built for the SFD in the '70s. It pulls a tillered trailer with a 100 foot aerial.

This 1959 Maxim with 75 foot stick is still a front-line piece in the town of Freetown, Massachusetts. It's been maintained impeccably, and it still goes downtown and does the job.

Here the crew is setting up for ladder pipe operations at a big mill fire in Taunton, Massachusetts.

Honolulu has a few straight ladder trucks, but they're not about to give up on their open-seat tillers. Ladder 7, pictured, covers the beaches and highrise hotels of Waikiki. Note sailboard for surf rescues!

involves back-breaking pickwork, pulling down ceilings, opening walls, and dragging ruined furniture or merchandise into the street. It's exhausting, it's messy, and it goes on forever. Firefighters love fighting fires, but it's hard to find a jake who loves to overhaul. Firefighters all over America are known as "jakes," by the way; no one seems to know why.

Engines tend to be very much alike everywhere, but ladder trucks come in a variety of types and sizes. The classic fire

Baltimore runs an even mix of tillers and straight trucks, although the older articulated rigs are being slowly eclipsed. And so is the famous Baltimore white-and-orange paint scheme. All the city's new apparatus are being delivered in plain old red.

truck, to many, is the articulated hook-and-ladder, a tractor-trailer array with a tillerman who steers the rear axle. The typical tillered aerial sports a powered "stick" capable of reaching 100 feet above the street, and a collection of eight or ten hand ladders in varying lengths. Many departments, from San Francisco to Philadelphia, still swear by their tillered rigs; among other things, they're thought to be more maneuverable in tight neighborhoods.

But most cities have abandoned them, citing their expense and their alarming propensity to get involved in traffic accidents. Boston, for instance, was given a straight-chassis loaner in 1985 by a newish apparatus manufacturer called Emergency-One out of Ocala, Florida; it was a short little two-axle truck with a 95 foot stick. Although they had used nothing but tillers since the Great Fire of 1872, they were so impressed with the compact rig that they abandoned their tiller fleet forthwith. The BFD now has some 30 active and reserve E-One ladder rigs with 106 foot aerials and nary a tillerman in sight. San Francisco, on the other hand, has nothing but tillered sticks, and they show no sign of changing

San Francisco's trucks, like this Spartan/LTI assigned to Station 15, must be able to accelerate up the steepest streets in town. The SFFD runs 18 tillered aerials similar to this one, and no other types of trucks. Try throwing a hand ladder on these streets! Frisco truckmen actually carry custom-made blocks in different thicknesses for shimming their ladders.

43

This beautiful Pierce quint is operated by the tiny (seven men on duty) department in Emeryville, California, next to Oakland. The rig was custom-built to be manned and operated by a single firefighter. A radio-controlled hydrant valve gradually increases pressure from the water source so the driver can hook up and then control the hydrant from his position at the control panel.

The classic fire truck, to many, is the articulated hook-and-ladder, a tractor-trailer array with a tillerman who steers the rear axle.

---

over. At this writing Philadelphia is proudly taking delivery of five new Spartan/LTI tillers with 105 foot sticks.

The biggest controversy regarding modern ladder trucks, aside from the question of yea or nay to the tiller, is whether to hang a bucket at the end of the stick. Many departments swear by an enclosed cage that can hold as many as five persons or a 1000 pound gross weight. The bucket

Small suburban departments often have minimal resources to devote to a working fire. Here a single engine and truck attack a good job in the attic of an Orange County house, about twenty miles south of central Los Angeles. Other companies are responding from a distance. The photo was shot from the Goodyear blimp.

Boston ran nothing but tillers for years, until an upstart apparatus manufacturer called Emergency-One convinced Commissioner Leo Stapleton to try one of their little single-rear-axle sticks for six months. The skeptics were soon won over, and today the few remaining tillers are kept only as reserve pieces. The BFD runs 23 of these 106 foot ladder trucks plus a single E-One tower ladder. Another tower is in active reserve.

greatly facilitates window rescues; the typical victim is terrified, not surprisingly, about the prospect of stepping out onto a slippery ladder rung 80 feet above the concrete. A powered bucket can pluck several people from as many windows and ease them down to the street before going back up for more. Buckets are also fitted with pre-connected heavy nozzles with telescopic plumbing running down one side of the stick. These big monitors can put huge streams into specific windows with a minimum of set-up time.

Bucket aerials come in several styles. The whole thing began in the late '50s with Chicago's first Snorkels. Then-commissioner Robert Quinn, soon to be known in the fire business as "Snorkel Bob," got

Las Vegas' Truck 4 tries 50 feet worth of horizontal extension to check the efficacy of the powered jacks. The bucket can carry a gross weight of almost 1000 pounds. The yellow tank on the side of the ladder is a supplemental breathing system, which many aerials have built into the base of the aerial. With this system, crews operating from the bucket can supplement the air supplies in their personal tanks.

the idea from watching utility crews work on power lines with their truck-mounted cherry pickers. Why not put a bucket like that on a fire truck? Why not, indeed. The classic Chicago Snorkel was a jack-knife array with a 75 foot vertical reach. The first Snorkel, put together from commercial components in the CFD shops, had been in service only a few weeks when a horrible

The biggest controversy regarding modern ladder trucks, aside from the question of yea or nay to the tiller, is whether to hang a bucket at the end of the stick.

fire at a parochial school called Our Lady of The Angels killed more than 90 pupils and nuns. On TV news programs all over the world, people interested in the fire service saw a strange-looking articulated arm panning over the fire scene, its 1200gpm Stang nozzle playing a heavy stream on the ruins. The CFD was flooded with calls from other departments: What the hell is the story on that rig with the cherry picker?

Snorkels are viewed with considerably less favor today, although Chicago and a few other big departments remain loyal to the technology. The big problem is the care that must be taken with the pesky elbow—it always seems to be banging into windows and wires across the street from the fire building. The rigs are also mechanically complex, maintenance-intensive, and prone to jams. But the biggest Snorkels offer tremendous reach. A triple-articulated version, designed in Finland by Bronto, can put a remote-controlled platform as high as 200 feet off the street. Bronto Skylifts of various dizzying heights are popular in Europe and Canada, but the 111 foot model in Bohemia, New York, mounted on a 1993 Pierce 10-wheel chassis, is to your writer's knowledge the only Bronto currently working in the United States.

Another popular variant of bucket tech-

nology is the tower ladder. This term can refer to any aerial appliance with a platform at the end, but it usually means the classic of the genre, the Baker Aerialscope. This is a bucket at the end of a stout, square telescoping tower. The Aerialscope isn't an aerial ladder truck; it has only a vestigial emergency ladder set into the top of the boom. New York has elevated the employment of the tower ladder to an art form. The FDNY operates about 75 of them, mostly mounted on Mack chassis, and their crews are expert at fast set-up, breathtaking bucket rescues, and surgical application of huge water streams from the ever-ready Stang nozzle. It's not uncommon for a big New York structure fire to fizzle in minutes once a single tower ladder finds the range and blasts 1000gpm in the window. Aerialscopes are popular in the mid-Atlantic states and New England, but they're seldom seen elsewhere in America. In New York they comprise about half of the ladder fleet, with nonarticulated aerials and a dwindling handful of tillered hook-and-ladders making up the other half.

Another interesting development, emanating from the always-innovative Phoenix Fire Department, is the ladder tender. This, simply put, is a ladder truck without ladders. Actually it carries a couple of small ground ladders and all the tools associated with ladder work, but no big, expensive powered appliance. The ladder tender idea grew from the realization that at many incidents, ranging from house fires to vehi-

cle accidents, the ladder crews have no use for the aerial. Ladder tenders are physically small, cheap to buy, and far cheaper and safer to operate on a per-mile basis. Phoenix and Tucson figure that their tenders run for about one-third the cost of a full-blown tiller. Seattle and many other cities once used and later abandoned several versions of the aerial-less ladder tender; these were commonly known as "city service" trucks.

A word about quads and quints at this point. These combination rigs can work as both engines and trucks—simultaneously, if need be. Most quint combinations have a pre-plumbed nozzle on the stick, and it can be supplied in short order from the rig's own pump and/or booster tank. Classic tower ladders like the Baker have no pump; they must be supplied by an engine. It's difficult for a single quint to have all the capabilities of both a full-sized engine and a full-sized ladder truck, but the best-designed of them come close. These combinations appeal mostly to small departments with few employees, but there are exceptions. One of San Francisco's 41 engines has been turned into a quad with

Left
Chicago's Truck 10 puts serious water onto a 5-11 job (the CFD's version of a fifth alarm). This Emergency-One tower has no internal pump or tank; it must be fed from an engine through its nose intake. Chicago has every type of ladder truck imaginable: tillers, straight sticks, towers, and its beloved Snorkels. *Larry Shapiro photo*

It's not uncommon for a big New York structure fire to fizzle in minutes once a single tower ladder finds the range and blasts 1000 gpm in the window.

the addition of several ground ladders (all made of hardwood, in the traditional Frisco mode) and a fifth crewperson. This rig, Engine 20, is first-due at a large old persons' home, and it has to be able to ladder the four-story structure before the first aerial, running from a distance, arrives and sets up. St. Louis is a good-sized urban department that has taken the unusual step of assigning quints, with either 50 foot or 75 foot powered aerials, to all of its 30 engine companies. These engines are all equipped with truck tools, including Hurst powered extraction systems (the "Jaws of Life"), and their crews are cross-trained for both pump and truck work. In addition several of the department's full-sized ladder trucks are also quints, with 1500gpm pumps and booster tanks as well as 110 foot rear-mount aerial ladders. St. Louis was thus able to eliminate four ladder companies while maintaining satisfactory truck coverage on all boxes.

The Orleans Street 5-11 finally darkens down, after the loss of a dozen large buildings. CFD

Tower Ladders 10 and 21 are being supplied by Engine 42, center. *Larry Shapiro photo*

The search and rescue side of the truckman's life is pretty glamorous, but roof venting is nothing but hard work. Here San Francisco truckmen use axes and power saws to vent the roof of a fully involved house. Ladder crews need to be constantly aware of a safe way out in case the roof starts to feel spongy. The battalion chief backed these firefighters off immediately after this shot was taken, due to the danger of collapse.

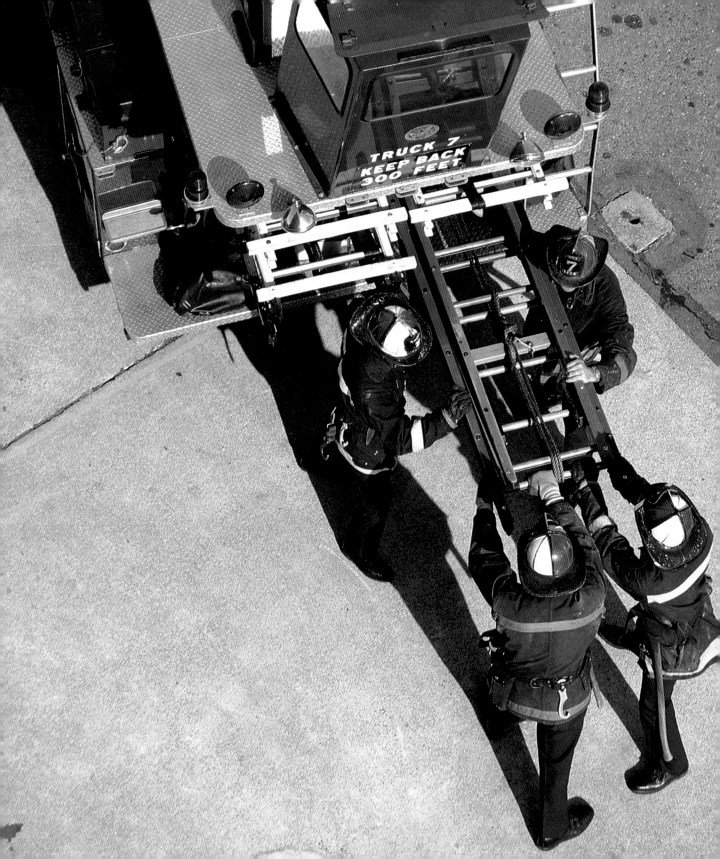

Bronx tower ladder 58 goes to work with a master stream. FDNY towers are famous for their ability to bludgeon fires in minutes with all the water in the world, perfectly placed. The local fire buffs hate the towers—they knock down the jobs too fast!

Left
Visiting firefighters are always amazed at the sight of San Francisco's heavy hardwood ladders. The department sticks with them partly out of tradition and partly because of the high-voltage trolley wires so prevalent in the city. A slip with a metal ladder could be fatal to a whole truck crew. The ladders are handmade by artisans at the city shops. San Francisco is also one of the few western departments sticking with Cairns leather helmets. Engine crews wear black, while truckmen sport the red-and-white motif.

New York has elevated the employment of the tower ladder to an art form . . .; [the] crews are expert at fast set-up, breathtaking bucket rescues, and surgical application of huge water streams from the ever-ready Stang nozzle.

Above

Boston runs lots of trucks—25 at last count. Only two have buckets, the front-line Tower Unit and the active reserve piece. The Tower Unit is an Emergency-One 100-footer with internal pump and tank. It responds to all working fires citywide to provide precision master streams. A second relief tower is also kept with this rig at Station 10 downtown, and it can be brought to a big job by personnel of the Motor Unit (equipment maintenance). *John Cetrino photo*

The suburban town of Kentfield north of San Francisco runs this cute little White snub-nose truck with an 85 foot stick. The rig is only partially manned, the crew counting on volunteers to take up the slack. Here the vollies get ready to vent the roof at a job in an auto dealership.

Tower ladder buckets feature pre-plumbed nozzles that can pump out 1000gpm only minutes after arrival on the scene. Ladder pipes are a more cumbersome way of putting out high-altitude master streams. They must be installed on the ladder's top rung and hooked to a big line running down the aerial. They must then be operated by a truckmen on the ladder. Some modern ladders have remote-controlled guns permanently installed at or near the top rungs. Here a tower gun and a ladder pipe both slug away at a Yonkers apartment job.
Tom Wanstall photo

The city of Lawrence, just northwest of Boston, is a dying mill town with the highest fire load per capita in America. Hundreds of major arson blazes have plagued the exhausted city in the past five years, and at least a couple of its many vacant buildings go up every week. A federal grant helped buy this new truck, a 95 foot Pierce Snorkel. *John Cetrino photo*

The Mack/Baker Aerialscope tower ladder doing what it does best. Powered center stabilizers, called tormentors, allow for quick set-up. The bucket crew can get in close and spot the best targets for their master stream. Ladder atop the tower is seldom used, as it is very narrow. It is primarily for emergency egress from the bucket in case of mechanical problems. *Tom Wanstall photo*

A ladder pipe, with low-tech remote control by ropes from the ground, lays a stream onto what's left of a lumber warehouse in Stoughton southeast of Boston. It's better than standing around and doing nothing, but not by much.

San Francisco's Truck 1 has laddered the roof of
the fire building immediately upon arrival, and
now the firefight has turned into an outside
attack with ladder pipes and heavy 3in lines.

Right
Creative ladder work on the back side of San
Francisco's Telegraph Hill. Other cities where hills
pose a major firefighting problem are Pittsburgh,
Seattle, and Rochester. And these towns have a
little something extra that San Francisco doesn't
have to worry about—ice and snow.

Chapter 3

Rescue

Left
Philadelphia's sole Heavy Rescue company runs to working fires city-wide in its handsome new Saulsbury rig. Normal rescue crew in Philly is an officer and five firefighters.

The civilian fire department on the Yuma, Arizona, Marine Corps Air Station provides structure fire coverage with five rigs including this all-wheel-drive heavy rescue built by Pierce. Active-duty Marine firefighters man the eight Oshkosh crash rigs in the runway side of the main fire station.

The Providence Fire Department's Special Hazards 1 serves as heavy rescue, water emergency and hazardous materials responder. Gear includes air bags for jacking, power saws, lights, vertical rescue equipment, BLS (basic life support) medical supplies, an inflatable boat, exposure suits, and a lot more, including the spectacular Hurst "Jaws of Life" extrication system (pictured center bottom). Its hydraulic power can be directed into either of two main tools, the cutter or the spreader. A wrecked car can literally be snipped into pieces to remove a trapped victim. *Mike Delaney photo*

The town of Taunton, Massachusetts, runs this new Emergency-One rescue squad built on a Ford L8000 diesel chassis. The enclosed rig is also set up with radios, phones and computer so it can function as a command post in fire, accident and hazmat situations.

Many rescue companies have primarily a medical function. Coral Gables, Florida, runs these three-man International rescue boxes that can also transport patients in a pinch. The crews are all cross-trained as both firefighters and EMTs. In addition, many of the CGFD's rescue officers are qualified to respond with the police SWAT team on hostage and shots-fired incidents.

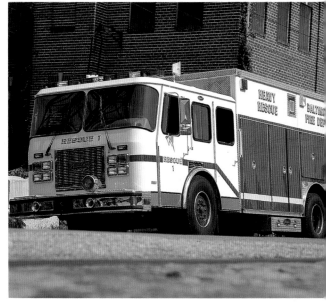

Right
Baltimore's brand-new Heavy Rescue is an Emergency-One box in the city's new red-and-white paint scheme. Baltimore's odd but lovable orange-under-white paint jobs will soon be a thing of the past.

Fans of the old EMERGENCY TV show remember the two-man rescue squads staffed by a pair of firefighter-paramedics. Few cities deploy this combination today, as the units have limited capabilities. Southern Marin County, just across the Golden Gate bridge from San Francisco, still dispatches this unit on all serious medical calls; it accompanies a BLS (basic life support) ambulance, and it always goes out with two fully qualified paramedic/firefighters. In additional to medical equipment the little rig is jammed with heavy rescue tools, including a Hurst Jaws of Life kit and rappeling gear for rope rescues.

Left
This 1958 Seagrave still serves the San Francisco Fire Department as a relief rescue, although it's soon bound for the city's superb fire museum located at Station 10. Built in a day when fire rigs looked like fire rigs, "Nellie Belle" is powered by a gasoline V-12. Here it flies up the ultra-steep Hyde Street hill (note cable car tracks and Alcatraz in the distance). Only a handful of SFFD drivers can deal with its cranky nonsynchro stick shift.

This mother of all heavy rescues was recently delivered to Aberdeen, Maryland. A Spartan chassis with bodywork by the rescue experts at Saulsbury, it sports a powered crane than can lift up to 13 tons. Phoenix has a similar crane installation on its principal rescue.
Joel Woods photo

Chapter 4

Airport Rigs

Left
This Oshkosh was rebuilt by Crash Rescue Equipment Service of Dallas as a rapid intervention unit for Phoenix Sky Harbor. It's now designated a CRE/CAV-2000, and its 10-man elevated cab can also be used as an on-scene command post. The handsome rig also carries 2,000 gallons of water and 1,000 gallons of dry foam.

Oshkosh is the big name in the specialized field of aircraft crash rescue vehicles. The awesome eight-wheel model M-12 is the big daddy. These rigs carry up to 5,000 gallons of water and foam in various combinations. Tucson's M-12 is a rarity in its deep red paint job; most airport rigs are lime green or bright yellow.

The Oshkosh M-12 at Phoenix Sky Harbor airport lets fly with two turret guns, both remote-controlled from inside the cab. The roof gun can blow out more than 2400gpm of water or foam.

Right
Phoenix's smaller Oshkosh T-12 is fitted with a powered "Snozzle" water tower that can actually penetrate the skin of a burning airliner and shoot water or foam inside.

These Emergency-One/Ford quick response vehicles can handle smaller airport incidents with extreme speed. Rigs carry Halon suppressant and dry chemicals rather than heavy water supplies. Jacksonville airport firefighters handle emergencies on the civilian side of the field, where the airliners come and go, and on the Air National Guard ramp where the weekend warriors operate a wing of F-16 Falcon fighters.

Left
Boeing's Paine airfield at Everett, Washington, is the birthplace of all 747 and 767 airliners; the new 777 jumbo will come off the line in 1995. Each new airliner undergoes almost a month of test-flying before delivery. The Paine crash fleet includes this Oshkosh T-3000.

Hickam Air Force Base, Honolulu, runs two
gigantic Oshkosh P-15 crash rigs with front and
rear high-volume turrets.

Left
Airport firefighters drill with a fire of burning fuel.
Airports and military bases use contaminated fuel,
usually ruined by water leakage, for firefighting
practice.

Chapter 5

Special Call

There's more to modern urban firefighting than engine and truck work. Most departments run a collection of single-use rigs that handle the ancillary jobs like heavy rescue, medical care, communications, lighting, toxic cleanup, and incident command. Some are regularly due on first alarm responses, while others roll only when they are special-called to the incident.

Rescue squads are common in departments large and small, but there are many different ways of employing these uniquely trained companies. Heavy rescues in the New York mold are operated by Atlanta, Boston, Denver, San Francisco, Honolulu, and a few dozen other departments. These are firefighting companies, running in heavily laden compartmentalized vans, that are trained and equipped for a score of potential emergency situations. Their pri-mary use is as highly experienced shock troops in the firefight. As their name implies, they enter the fire building to conduct primary and secondary searches for victims and evacuees. With everyone safely out, the rescuemen usually help with truck-work on the roof, although in some departments they will take the lead on the attack hose lines (and you can just imagine how thrilled the engine guys are about handing the nob over to these prima donnas!). Rescue squads in big departments are invariably elite units; the crews and their officers decide who can make the team, and they only accept people with experience, aggres-

The Phoenix Fire Department's Emergency-One command post responds on all working fires. Chief officers supervise the firefight from its air-conditioned interior—no small consideration in a place as infernally hot as Phoenix. Rig is manned fulltime by a driver/operator.

siveness, and special skills. And, as they used to say at Rescue 3 in the Bronx, extra points for a metal plate in your head.

Rescue companies also handle nonfire emergencies such as vehicle accidents, collapses, hillside saves, and industrial injuries. A fire department rescue squad usually packs a high degree of medical expertise, with firefighters who have undergone EMT and paramedic training at various levels. It's also common for these units to be trained and equipped for water rescues, using SCUBA gear, small boats, and lifelines. New York runs five heavy rescues, one in each borough, and the companies have subdivided their responsibilities. Two have water-rescue training and gear, another two are specially equipped to handle building collapses, three are tasked to han-

dle subway and train disasters, and so on. The FDNY faces a unique problem with regard to nonfire rescues: it's the only large American city in which the police maintain primary responsibility for much emergency rescue work. Their Emergency Service Units take charge at most vehicle accidents, for instance, and the coppers are zealous, to put it mildly, when it comes to holding the firefighters at an arm's length. Firefighters have actually been arrested and cuffed at accident scenes on New York expressways by ESU cops insistent on handling the rescue unaided.

Heavy rescues carry industrial-strength entry tools, ropes and cables for vertical rescues, a selection of power saws, and various hydraulic systems for serious cutting, prying, and jacking. The Hurst "Jaws of Life" tool is actually a combination of devices connected to a powerful hydraulic compressor. The spreader attachment can be used to pop open jammed car doors, and the cutting blades will slice through steel side pillars so that a flattened car roof can be snipped and lifted away in one piece. Another hydraulic tool is a system of steel-reinforced air bags of different sizes that can be used as inflatable jacks to lift dead weights as heavy as railroad cars or fully loaded truck trailers.

Smaller rescues, running with crews of two or three, are primarily medical response units. Some are set up as full-service ambulances that can transport victims under ALS (advanced life support) condi-

Phoenix command van interior during a working high-rise incident.

The mother of all command vans is this monster fielded by Orange County Fire Rescue in Florida. It can communicate on every frequency used in the state, including military, amateur, and even satellite channels. Trailer is towed by a 1990 Freightliner tractor. Confusion and miscommunication in the wake of south Florida's Hurricane Andrew formed the impetus for the development of this amazing rig.

Most departments of any size operate an air service unit to keep breathing bottles and oxygen systems filled up. These trucks also carry several dozen extra bottles that can be put to work at a big job. Usually the mask service unit responds automatically on any second alarm or working fire. Pictured is Baltimore's new cascade unit.

Left
Phoenix can supplement its new Emergency-One lighting plant with a gaggle of small lighting trailers. The little trailers can be left in operation at a fire scene while the towing vehicle goes on to other duties.

tions. Firefighting is strictly a secondary responsibility for these crews.

Other departments combine rescue and hazardous-materials duties in a single outfit. The Special Hazards Unit of the busy Providence, Rhode Island, Fire Department rolls in an ultra-sophisticated Pemfab rig with bodywork by Ranger. The company is equally adept with fire attack, rescues, water emergencies and toxic clean-ups. Included in the rig's inventory are chemical-protection suits, one-hour breathing apparatus for all hands, and an on-board computer with data bases on every chemical and industrial mishap known to man. Special Hazards is also due on every working fire ("Code Red" in Providence parlance) in the city limits.

Single-function trucks are necessary in departments of any size. These units make their appearance at multiple alarms or complex incidents. Air supply or cascade vans contain spare breathing bottles plus an on-board compressor to fill tanks as fast as they are depleted. These rigs also provide pure oxygen to engines and rescues for medical resuscitations. They usually make regular delivery runs to each firehouse to drop off full bottles and to maintain the

Rural departments often supplement their engine forces with one or more tankers. These trucks can carry several thousand gallons of water to a remote location where fire hydrants are inadequate or nonexistent. Some can also pump; most can only lead to an engine, which in turn takes care of pumping the water onto the fire. This is the "Water Works," run by the volunteers in Evergreen, Virginia. *Joel Woods photo*

masks and resuscitators. Lighting plants can illuminate night fire scenes, and they also contain powerful AC generators that can turn up as much as 30 kilowatts of juice. The always-thinking Phoenix Fire Department got the brilliant idea of buying several small lighting trailers, just like the ones seen at road construction sites, and towing them to emergency scenes where they can be left chugging away while the towing vehicle (lighting truck or rescue squad) goes back into service. The little trailers work great, and they're cheap—about $10,000 each with self-contained gas generator and a spiffy red paint job.

Many departments send command and communication vans to big fires, so that the firefight can be supervised from a comfortable and quiet environment. The rigs are set up with banks of radios, cellular phones, fax machines, and computers detailing all of the city's building types and land uses. Many carry radio repeaters that can substitute for the city-wide systems to provide more solid communications within a few hundred yards of the fire building. Phoenix again has one of the best command units around, an expensively outfitted Emergency-One command post. The big daddy of this genre is undoubtedly the immense tractor-trailer rig fielded by the Orange County, Florida, fire department. The devastation of recent hurricanes led to the development and construction of this beautiful super-rig.

Other units are outfitted to handle only

Fireboats are engines too! Big, big engines, to be exact. San Francisco's *Phoenix* was widely heralded as the savior of the city after the 1989 earthquake; its pumps got seawater onto several fires a half mile from the shore in the Marina District. The boat can move 8000gpm through several deck guns and outflow valves. The SFFD's second fireboat, the larger *Guardian,* was given anonymously to the city by a grateful citizen after the big quake. It had previously served Vancouver, British Columbia. The *Phoenix* is manned fulltime by a skipper and engineer; on fire runs it takes on the crew of Engine 35, with which it shares bayside quarters.

a specific type of emergency. Since Boston is in the midst of several big federally funded tunnel projects, they have put into service two Emergency-One tunnel and trench collapse trucks, and a number of downtown ladder companies have been trained in their use. The feds have also bought Boston a brand-new Emergency- One heavy rescue (as you may have guessed, Boston has for the last decade fielded nothing but E-One equipment), to be quartered at downtown Station 10. New York runs a building collapse truck on the same basis; two rescue squads and several ladder companies respond with it to urban collapses or subway disasters.

Aircraft fires pose such unique problems that most cities have separate departments to handle crash emergencies. In some cases these companies are a division of the city department, and in other situations, such as Boston and New York, they are administered by separate port authorities. Federal regulations dictate the equipment specifications and manpower training for most airport departments. The firefighting problems are formidable: the units must respond with tremendous speed, and they must be prepared to launch extremely aggressive attacks immediately upon arrival. The engines have to accelerate and brake like sports cars, despite having to carry huge water and foam supplies on board; there are no hydrant systems on most airfields. The biggest Oshkosh 8-wheel crash rigs, powered by 550hp blown diesels, have internal tanks that can lug 5000 gallons of water—that's 14 tons—plus another 500

Good-looking "Hummer" brushfire truck is an impressive performer, but it's fiendishly expensive—about twice as much as a comparable all-wheel-drive pickup.

gallons of AFFF (aqueous film-forming foam) in 3 percent or 6 percent solution. With petroleum fires, which airport crews must be prepared to face, foam gives far better cooling and smothering performance. Airport rigs accelerate like crazy and nose right into the flames, spouting water and foam from remote-controlled monitors on the roof and front bumper. They can also put hand lines to work, moved forward by firefighters in fireproof gear.

The typical airport department also has several small attack rigs with pumps and tanks mounted on four-wheel drive pickup chassis. These little pumpers can deal with common aircraft incidents like blown tires and burning brakes. Very similar rigs are also used to fight brush fires in many urban departments. The folks who make the Army's "Hummer," the big diesel Jeep of the '90s, are fielding a couple of fire-fighting versions for use in field and swamp scenarios. They look great, but their price tags are daunting. Few have been sold thus far.

Chief officers usually respond to fires in dedicated vehicles. Some departments expect their chiefs to drive, but the preferred deployment is with an aide at the wheel. That way the driver can worry exclusively about traffic while responding Code 3 (full lights and siren), and the chief can monitor radio communications to stay abreast of the developing incident.

In San Francisco, the West's most tradi-tion-bound department, chiefs' sedans are still referred to by one and all as "buggies," and aides are known as "operators." Until the 1940s the chief's operator linked the incident to central fire alarm via a tele-graph key inside the corner fire box, and the term has stuck.

Most cities mount their chiefs in full-size sedans set up with police suspensions and heavy-duty electrical and cooling systems. Chief and aide keep breathing apparatus, spare radios, and lights in the trunk, but not much else in the way of equipment. New York and many other departments now install mobile video terminals, or MVTs, in the front seat to provide the chief with computer-generated data on the units due and the specifics of the fire building.

New York is also credited with starting the move toward big, bad chiefs' cars. In the 1970s the FDNY stuck its chiefs and aides in lightweight Chrysler K-cars, but after several terrible intersection accidents, one of them fatal to a battalion chief, the rolling-stock mavens gave up on that money-saving scheme. They started buying four-wheel-drive Chevy Suburbans, huge station wagons that are more truck than car. They ordered them with V-8 diesels, so they could refuel from firehouse storage tanks, and they've never looked back. The big 'Burbans are like tanks in traffic, and they're also useful as utility vehicles with their seating for eight. Many other cities from Minneapolis to Seattle have picked up on the idea.

Chapter 6

Coats of Many Colors

We all agree, of course, that American fire apparatus should be red and red alone. It's amazing to behold the number of cities and departments that don't agree. Rigs come in every color imaginable, with new hues showing up all the time.

There was a widespread flirtation in the '70s with a bilious lime yellow or chartreuse, first introduced by apparatus manufacturer Ward LaFrance, that was thought to yield better nighttime visibility. Some departments have stuck with it, and the federal aviation types still prefer it for airport crash rigs. But most departments ran screaming from the experiment, and today it's hard to find many examples of this dreaded color. The current wisdom holds that red with some sort of reflective white or yellow striping has even better nighttime visibility properties. The Boston Fire Department suffered through a long winter of the soul in the early 1980s, when mayoral corruption, personnel layoffs, and an unprecedented wave of malicious arson pounded the outfit to its knees. This self-same mayor ordered all BFD apparatus painted a particularly monstrous shade of green-yellow, supposedly selected by his wife (an apocryphal tale, perhaps). When a new mayor and the beloved Commissioner Leo Stapleton arrived on the scene to repair the damage in 1984, one of Stapie's first orders was: back to red, boys. Morale soared instantly.

The Occupational Safety and Health Administration (OSHA), is now leading the charge back to red—ironic, of course, since

This new Quality engine was delivered to Clearwater, Florida, in "German Red," a day-glo paint that tends toward the orange. It screams out at night when lit by other headlights.

One of Baltimore's two super-stations, with engines, truck, heavy rescue, ambulance, and chief's Cherokee all sporting the famous orange-and-white scheme. New Baltimore rigs are showing up in handsome but boring red.

chartreuse was partly their idea in the first place. There are lots of different reds at work, from classic "fire engine red" in the middle to near-orange at one end and maroon at the other. San Francisco has stuck with its unique deep red since the '30s, while the newest development is so-called "German Red," a day-glo version of red popular in Europe. It's hot, all right. You can check it out in Clearwater, Florida, among other places.

Bright white and various yellows from pale to taxicab are popular and not unattractive. Volunteer outfits tend to roam far afield with oddball greens, blues, violets, and even black! Chicago is sticking with its famous black tops over red, and Philadelphia is joining Jacksonville, Florida, in adapting a red-with-gold-stripes combo. Baltimore, sadly, is giving up on its wonderfully eccentric orange-and-white scheme in favor of OSHA-sanctioned red. That leaves Springfield, Oregon, as the only department still staying with unapologetic orange. Their new Pierce quint looks especially spiffy with its navy blue accent stripe.

Unless your author is misinformed, Springfield, Oregon, is the last department anywhere running all-orange apparatus. The little department runs Pierce equipment exclusively, including this 1990 Pierce Arrow engine with 750-gallon booster tank and a rehab 1972 Pierce/Oshkosh 85 foot Snorkel truck. This rig is a duplicate of the classic Chicago Snorkels.

The Marines painted these Oshkoshes for use in Desert Storm, and they're in no hurry to change them back to god-awful chartreuse. The red-suited driver is active-duty Marine trained in airport firefighting.

Glenn Dale, Maryland, is the lucky owner of this beautiful deep yellow Spartan rescue, bodywork by Marion. *Joel Woods photo.*

We all agree, of course, that American fire apparatus should be red and red alone. . . [but] rigs come in every color imaginable, with new hues showing up all the time.

Washington, DC, runs this 102 foot tower ladder built by Grumman. The red-white-and-star motif is found throughout the department. This truck is due on first alarms at the White House.
Joel Woods photo

Why not green, especially when your town is called Long Green? The beautiful 1991 Emergency-One has a 1250gpm pump and an oversized (1,300 gallons) booster tank for brush work. *Joel Woods Photo*

If green is good to go, why not blue? Actually, blue was a common color for fire apparatus around the time of World War II. Still an active-duty unit, this magnificently maintained 1940 Ford/Howe runs as a small pump (400gpm) and as a lighting plant in Walkersville, Maryland. *Joel Woods photo*

Left

And if green and blue are OK, why not black? The only black rig your author has seen, this Baker Aerialscope 95 foot tower ladder was one of the last built. It runs as Tower 7 in Riverdale, Maryland. *Joel Woods photo*

Another good-looking pumper-tanker combo, built by Grumman in 1990. Light yellow with white scheme is easy on the eyes. Operated by Roanoke County, Virginia. *Joel Woods photo*

Index